石黑一雄诺贝尔奖获奖演说

我的二十世纪之夜及其他小突破

（中英双语）

Kazuo Ishiguro Nobel Lecture

My Twentieth Century Evening – and Other Small Breakthroughs

〔英〕石黑一雄 著　宋佥 译

上海译文出版社

石黑一雄作品

KAZUO ISHIGURO

《长日将尽》《莫失莫忘》《我辈孤雏》《无可慰藉》
《浮世画家》《被掩埋的巨人》《远山淡影》《小夜曲》

石黑一雄，日裔英国小说家，1954年生于日本长崎。1989年获得"布克奖"，与奈保尔、拉什迪并称"英国文坛移民三雄"，2017年获诺贝尔文学奖。

石黑一雄诺贝尔奖获奖演说

我的二十世纪之夜及其他小突破

如果你在一九七九年的秋天遇见我，你会发现你很难给我定位，不论是社会定位还是种族定位。我那时二十四岁。我的五官很日本。但与那个年代大多数你在英国碰见的日本男人不同，我长发及肩，还留着一对弯弯的悍匪式八字须。从我讲话的口音里，你唯一能够分辨出的就是：我是一个在英国南方长大的人，时而带着一抹懒洋洋的、已经过时的嬉皮士腔调。如果我们得以交谈，我们也许会讨论荷兰的全攻全守足球队，或者是鲍勃·迪伦的最新专辑，或者是刚刚过去的一年里我在伦敦帮助无家可归者的经历。如果你提起日本，问我关于日本文化的问题，你也许会在我的态度中察觉到一丝不耐烦——我会宣称我对此一无所知，因为我自从五岁那年离开日本起，就再未踏足那个国度——甚至都没有回去度过一次假。

那年秋天，我背着一个旅行包，带着一把吉他和一台便携式打字机，来到了诺福克郡的巴克斯顿——一个英国小村庄，有着一座古老的水磨坊，四周是一片平坦的农田。我之所以来到这里，是因为我被东英吉利大学的一个创造性写作研究生课程所录取，学时一年。那所大学就在十英里外，在主教座堂所在的诺威奇市，但我没有汽车，所以我去那里的唯一途径就是搭乘一趟只有早、中、晚三班的巴士。但我很快发现，这一点并没有给我带来多少麻烦：我一般一周只需去学校两次。我在一栋小房子里租了一个房间，房主是一个三十多岁的男人，他的妻子刚刚离他而去。

无疑，于他而言，这栋房子充斥着破碎旧梦的幽灵——但也许他只是不想见我吧；总之，我经常一连数天都不见他的踪影。换句话说，在经历了那段疯狂的伦敦岁月后，我来到了这里，直面这超乎寻常的清幽与寂寞，而我正是要在这幽寂中将自己变成一个作家。

事实上，我的小房间确实很像经典的作家阁楼。天花板的坡度之陡简直要让人得幽闭恐惧症——尽管我踮起脚尖，就能透过一扇窗户看见大片的耕田无尽地延伸到远方。房间里有一张小桌子，桌面几乎被我的打字机和一盏台灯完全占满了。地板上没有床，只有一大块长方形的工业泡沫塑料，拜它所赐，我在睡梦中没少流汗，哪怕是在诺福克那些冰冷刺骨的夜晚。

正是在这个房间里，我认真审读了我夏天完成的两个短篇小说，思忖着它们究竟够不够格，可不可以提交给我的新同学们。（据我所知，我们班级里有六个人，两周碰一次头。）我到那时为止还没有写过多少值得一提的小说类作品，能够被研究生课程录取全凭一部被BBC退稿的广播剧。事实上，在此之前，我二十岁的时候就已经定下了成为摇滚歌星的明确打算，我的文学志向是直到不久前才浮上心头的。我此刻审视的两个短篇是慌乱之中匆匆草就的，因为我那时刚刚得知自己被大学写作课程录取了。其中一篇写的是一个可怕的自杀契约，另一篇写的是苏格兰的街头斗殴——我在苏格兰做过一段时间的社工。这两篇写得都不好。于是我另开新篇，这次写一名少年毒死了自己的猫，背景同样设定在当今的英国。然后，一天晚上，在我待在那个小房间里的第三或是第四周，我发现自己开始以一种全新的、紧迫的热情写起了日本——写起了长崎，我出生的那座城市——在二战最后的那些日子。

这件事，我需要指出，对当时的我来说可谓出乎意料。今天，在当下盛行的文坛风气中，一位有多元文化背景、渴望成就一番事业的年轻作家几乎会本能地在创作中“寻根”。但那时的情况根本不是这样。我们距离“多元文化”在英国的大爆发还有几年光景。萨尔曼·拉什迪那时默默无闻，名下只有一部已经绝版的小说。那时你向别人问起当下最杰出的年轻英国作家，得到的回答很可能是玛格丽特·德拉布尔；至于老一辈的作家，则有艾丽丝·默多克、金斯利·艾米斯、威廉·戈尔丁、安东尼·伯吉斯、约翰·福尔斯。像加夫列尔·加西亚·马尔克斯、米兰·昆德拉、博尔赫斯这样的外国人只有极小众的读者，即便是阅读面颇广的人也对他们的名字毫无印象。

当时的文坛风气就是这样。因此，当我完成了首个关于日本的短篇时，尽管我感觉自己发现了一个重要的新方向，心中却也不免随即升起了一层疑云，不知这场冒险究竟算不算是一种自我放纵——也不知我究竟是否应该赶快回到“正常”的题材轨道上来。我再三犹豫之后，才开始将这篇作品分发给大家看；直到今日，我依然深深地感激我的同学们，感激我的两位导师——马尔科姆·布拉德伯里与安吉拉·卡特，感激小说家保罗·贝利——他是当年的大学驻校作家，感激他们对我这部作品坚定的鼓励。如果他们的反应不是那么正面的话，也许我就再也不会碰任何有关日本的题材了。但我是幸运的。我回到房间里，开始写啊写。一九七九年到一九八〇年的那整个冬天，连带着半个春天，除了班里的五位同学，村里的食品杂货店老板（我仰赖他的早餐麦片和羊腰子为生），还有我的女朋友洛娜（如今是我的太太）——她每两周就会在周末来看我一次——我几乎不跟任何人说话。这样的生活有失平衡，但在那四五个月里，我的头一部长篇小说——《远山淡影》——完成了一半。这部作品同样设置在长崎，在原子弹落下后从核爆中走出的那些岁月。我记得，这段时期我也曾动过念头，想创作几篇不以日本为背景的短篇小说，却发现自己对此很快意兴阑珊。

那几个月对我来说至关重要——如果不是因为这段经历，我可能永远也不会成为一名作家。从那以后，我经常回首往事，不断地问自己：我这是怎么啦？这股奇特的力量究竟从何而来？我的结论是，在我生命中的那一个节点，我忽然全身心投入一项急切的“保存”工作。要解释这一点，我就得把时钟再往前拨。

*

一九六〇年四月，也就是我五岁那年，我随父母同姐姐一道来到萨里郡的吉尔福德镇，这里位于伦敦以南三十英里的那片富裕的“股票经纪人聚居区”。我的父亲是一位科学研究人员——一位前来为英国政府工作的海洋学家。顺便提一句，他后来发明的机器成为了伦敦科学博物馆的永久藏品。

我们到来不久后拍摄的照片展现的是一个已经消逝的英国。男人们穿着V字领羊毛套衫，打着领带，汽车上依然有踏板，车后面挂着一个备胎。披头士，性革命，学生抗议活动，“多元文化主义”全都即将到来，但很难想象我们全家初遇的那个英国对此有半点预感。碰见一个从法国或意大利来的外国人已经够了不得了——更别提从日本来的了。

我们家住在一条由十二栋房子组成的死巷中，这里刚好是水泥道路的终点与乡村郊野的起点。

从这里只需步行不到五分钟，就能来到一片当地的农场，还有成队的奶牛沿着田间小径来回跋涉。牛奶是靠马车配送上门的。我初来英国的那些日子里，有一道屡见不鲜的景观是我直到今日还清楚记得的，那就是刺猬——这些漂亮可爱、浑身是刺的夜行生灵那时在乡间到处都是；夜间，它们被车轮轧扁，遗留在了晨露中，然后被干净利落地码在路边，等待着清洁工来收走。

我们所有的邻居那时都上教堂，我去找他们的孩子玩耍时，我注意到他们吃饭前都要说一句简短的祷词。

我进了主日学校，很快就加入了唱诗班；到我十岁时，我成为了吉尔福德的首位日裔唱诗班领唱。我上了本地的小学——我是学校里唯一的外国学生，或许也是该校有史以来的唯一一位——到我十一岁时，我开始坐火车去上邻镇的一所文法学校，每天早上都会和许许多多穿着细条纹西装、戴着圆顶礼帽、赶往伦敦的办公室上班的男人们共享一节车厢。

到了这时，我已经完全掌握了那个年代的英国中产阶级孩子所应遵循的一切礼仪。去朋友家做客时，我知道一有成人进屋，我就要马上立正。我学会了在用餐时如果需要下桌，必须征得许可。作为街区里唯一的外国男孩，我在当地甚是出名，走到哪里都有人认得。其他孩子在遇见我之前就已经知道我是谁了。我完全不认识的陌生成年人有时会在大街上或是当地的小店里直呼我的名字。

当我回首那段经历，想起那时距离二战结束还不到二十年，而日本在那场大战中曾经是英国人的死敌时，我总是惊诧于这个平凡的英国社区竟以如此的开阔心胸与不假思索的宽宏大量接纳了我们一家。对于经历了二战，并在战后的余烬中建立起一个令人叹为观止的崭新福利国家的那代英国人，我心中永远保留着一份温情、敬意与好奇，直至今日，而这份情感很大程度上来源于我在那些年里的个人经历。

但与此同时，我在家中却又和我的日本父母一起过着另一种生活。家中，我面对的是另一套规矩，另一种要求，另一种语言。我父母最初的打算是，我们一年后就回日本，或者两年。事实上，我们在英国度过的头十一年里，我们永远都在准备着“明年”回国。因此，我父母的心态一直都是把自己看作旅居者而非移民。他们经常会交换对于当地人那些奇风异俗的看法，全然不觉有任何效法的必要。长久以来，我们一直认定我会回到日本开启我的成人生活，我们也一直努力维系我的日式教育。每个月，从日本都会寄来一个邮包，里面装着上个月的漫画、杂志与教育文摘，这一切我都如饥似渴地囫囵吞下。我十几岁时的某一天，忽然不再有日本来的邮包了——也许那是在我祖父去世之后——但我父母依然谈论着旧友、亲戚，还有他们在日本的生活片段，这一切都继续向我稳定地传输着画面与印象。另外，我一直都储藏着我自己的记忆——储量惊人地大，细节惊人地清晰：我记得我的祖父母，记得我留在日本的那些我最喜爱的玩具，记得我们住过的那栋传统日居（直到今日我依然能在脑海里将它逐屋重构出来）、我的幼儿园、当地的有轨电车站、桥下那条凶猛的大狗，还有理发店里那把为小男孩特制的椅子，大镜子前面有一个汽车方向盘。

这一切造成的结果就是，随着我逐渐长大，远在我动过用文字创造虚构世界的念头之前，我就已经忙不迭地在脑海里构建一个细节丰富、栩栩如生的地方了，而这个地方就叫做“日本”，那是我某种意义上的归属所在，从那里我获得了一种身份认同感与自信感。那段时间我的身体从未回过日本一次，但这一点反倒使得我对那个国度的想象更加鲜活，更加个人化。

而保存这一切的需求也就由此而来。因为，到了我二十五岁的时候，我渐渐得出了几个关键性的认识——尽管当时我从未清晰地将其付诸言语。我开始接受几个事实：也许“我的”日本并不与飞机能带我去的任何一个地方相吻合；也许我父母谈论的那种生活方式——我所记得的那种我幼年时的生活方式——已经在一九六〇年代和一九七〇年代基本消失了；无论如何，存在于我头脑中的那个日本也许只是一个孩子用记忆、想象和猜测拼凑起来的情感构建物。也许最重要的是，我开始意识到，随着我年齿渐长，我的这个日本——这个伴随我长大的宝地——正变得越来越模糊。

我不确定驱使我在诺福克的那间小屋里奋笔

疾书的究竟是不是这样一种情感——“我的”日本既独一无二，又极端脆弱，因为那是某种无法通过外界得到印证的东西。我所做的就是用纸和笔记下那个世界独特的色彩、道德观念、礼仪规范，记下它的尊严、它的缺陷，以及我对它所思所想的一切，赶在它们从我的脑海中消逝以前。我的愿望是，在小说中重建我的日本，保护它免遭破坏；从此以后，我就可以指着一本书，说：“是的。那里就是我的日本。就在那里。”

*

三年半后，一九八三年春，洛娜和我身处伦敦，住在一栋高高窄窄的房子顶楼的两个房间里，这房子本身又建在城市最高点之一的一座小山上。

那附近有一座电视信号塔，每当我们想要听唱片时，幽灵般的广播人声总是会时断时续地侵入我们的音箱。我们的客厅里没有沙发和扶手椅，只有放在地上的两个床垫，上面铺着软垫。房间里还有一张大桌子，白天我在上面写作，晚上我俩在上面吃饭。这居所不怎么奢华，但我们都很喜欢。前一年我刚出版了我的首部长篇小说，我还为一部电影短片写了剧本，短片很快就要在英国电视台播放了。

有一阵子，对于我的首部长篇我还是颇引以为豪的，但是到了那年春天，一种挠心般的不满感开始露头。问题出在这里：我的首部长篇和我的首个电视剧本太相似了。相似点不在于主题素材，而在于方法和风格。我越看这件事，就越觉得我的小说像是一个剧本——对白加上表演指导。某种程度上说，这一点并无大碍，但我此刻的愿望是创作一部只能以书页传达的小说。如果我的小说带给别人的体验与看电视大同小异，那么这样一部小说又有什么创作的必要呢？如果文字小说不能提供给读者某种独有的、其他媒介无法呈现的东西，那它又怎敢奢望能对抗电影和电视的力量呢？

就在这时，我害了一场病毒感染，卧床休息了几日。等到我挨过了病痛的高峰期，不再整天昏昏欲睡了，我发现被褥中折磨了我好一阵子的那件沉甸甸的东西居然是一本普鲁斯特的《追忆似水年华》第一卷（*Remembrance of Things Past*，当时的书名就是这么译的）。就这样，我开卷读了起来。我当时依然发着烧，这或许也是一个推波助澜的因素，但总之我被“序言”和“贡布雷”两部分完全迷住了。我读了一遍又一遍。除了这些章节本身纯粹的美感，我还为普鲁斯特从一个章节衔接到另一个章节的手法所倾倒。事件与场景的排列并不遵循通常的时间次序，也不遵循线性的情节发展。相反，发散的思绪联想，或是记忆的随性游走在章节与章节间推进着文字。有时，我发现自己在问这样的问题：这两个看似毫不相干的瞬间为何会在叙述者的头脑中并列出现？忽然间，我为我的下一部小说找到了一种激动人心、更加自由的创作方式——一种能够让丰富的色彩跃然纸上的创作方式，一种能够描绘出银幕无法捕捉的内心活动的创作方式。如果我也能够用叙述者的那种思维联想与记忆漂流在段落与段落间推进，我就能像一位抽象画家在画布上随心所欲地放置形状与色彩那样创作小说了。我能将两天前的一幕场景与二十年前的另一幕场景并置，请读者去思考两者间的联系。我开始思考，每个人对于自我和过去的认知都是笼罩在自我欺骗与否认真相的层层迷雾之中的，而这样一种创作方式也许能够助我揭示这一层又一层的迷雾。

*

一九八八年三月，我三十三岁。这时我们有了沙发，我正横躺在沙发上，听着一张汤姆·威兹的专辑。一年前，洛娜和我在南伦敦一个并不时尚但温馨惬意的城区中买下了我们自己的房子，而就在这栋房子里，头一次，我有了自己的书房。书房很小，连房门都没有，但能够把稿纸四处铺开，再不必每天晚上把手稿收好，这一点依然令我激动不已。正是在那间书房里——或者说，我相信是在那里——我刚刚完成了我的第三部长篇小说。这是我的第一部不以日本为背景的长篇——我的前两部作品已经让那个只属于我个人的日本不那么脆弱了。事实上，我的新书——我将为它取名《长日将尽》——乍看上去英国化得无以复加，尽管——这是我的希望——不是以老一辈英国作家的那种方式。我非常留意地提醒自己，不要预先假定——因为我知道，许多老一辈作家正是这样假定的——我的读者都是英国人，对于英式的微妙情感与执念烂熟于心。到了那时，萨尔曼·拉什迪与V·S·奈保尔这样的作家已经为一种更加国际化、更加面向外部世界的英国文学开辟了道路，这样一种新英国文学并不理所当然地将英国放在中心位置。他们的创作是最广泛意义上的后殖民文学。我也想像他们一样，写一部能够轻易穿越文化与语言边界的“国际”小说，与此同时却又将故事设定在一个英国独有的世界中。我这个版本的英国会是一个传说中的英国，它的轮廓，我相信，已经存在于全世界人民的想象之中了，包括那些从未踏足这个国度的人。

我刚刚完成的这个故事写的是一个英国管家，在人生的暮年，为时已晚地认识到他的一生一直遵循着一套错误的价值观；认识到他将自己的大好年华用来侍奉一个同情纳粹的人；认识到因为拒绝为自己的人生承担道德责任与政治责任，他在某种深层意义上浪费了人生。还有：在他追求成为完美仆人的过程中，他自我封闭了那扇爱与被爱的大门，阻绝了他自己与那个他唯一在意的女人。

我把手稿通读了几遍，感觉还算满意。不过，一种挠心感依然挥之不去：这里头还是缺了点什么。

就这样，如我所说，一天晚上，我躺在屋里的沙发上，听着汤姆·威兹。这时，汤姆·威兹唱起了一首叫做《鲁比的怀抱》的歌。也许你们当中有人听过这首歌。（我甚至想过要在此刻为你们唱上一曲，但最终我改了主意。）这首情歌唱的是一个男人，也许是一名士兵，将熟睡的爱人独自留在了床上。正值清晨，他一路前行，登上了火车。演唱者用的是美国流动工人的那种低沉粗哑的嗓音，完全不习惯表露自己的深层情感。这时，就在歌曲唱到半当中的时候，在那一刻，歌手突然告诉我们，他的心碎了。这一刻感人至深，让人几乎不可能不动容，而这份感动恰恰来自于一种张力，张力的一头是这种情感本身，另一头是为了宣告这份情感而不得不克服的巨大阻力。汤姆·威兹用一种飞流直下的宣泄唱出了这句歌词，你能感受到一个将情感压抑了一辈子的硬汉在无法战胜的伤悲面前终于低头了。

我一边听着汤姆·威兹，一边认识到了我还需要做什么。之前，我不假思索地做出了一个决定：我笔下的这位英国管家会坚守住自己的情感防线，躲在这道防线后面，既是躲避自己，也是躲避读者，直到全书告终。可现在，我知道我必须推翻这一决定。在某个时刻，在故事临近尾声时——一个我必须精心选择的时刻——我必须让他的盔甲裂开一道缝。我必须让他流露出一种巨大的、悲剧性的渴望——渴望有人能够窥见那盔甲之下的真容。

这里，我得说一句，除了这件事，我还不止一次地从歌手的声音中得到过其他至关重要的启迪。我在这里指的并不是唱出来的歌词，而是演唱本身。我们知道，歌唱的人声能够传达复杂得超乎想象的情感混合物。这些年来，我作品的某些细节方面尤其受到了鲍勃·迪伦、妮娜·西蒙娜、埃米卢·哈里斯、雷·查尔斯、布鲁斯·斯普林斯汀、吉利恩·韦尔奇，还有我的朋友兼合作者史黛西·肯特的影响。我从他们的声音中捕捉了某种东西，然后对自己说："啊，没错。就是这个。这就是我在这一幕中需要捕捉的东西。与之非常接近的东西。"那时常是一种我无法用文字表达的情感，但它确实就在那里，在歌手的声音里，而现在我得到了一个可以瞄准的目标。

*

一九九九年十月，我应德国诗人克里斯托夫·霍伊布纳代表国际奥斯威辛委员会之邀，参观了这座前集中营，并在这里度过了数日。我的居所安排在了奥斯威辛青年会议中心，就在第一座奥斯威辛集中营与两英里外的比克瑙死亡集中营之间的公路上。有人引领我遍访了这几处旧址，我在那里与三名幸存者进行了非正式的会面。我感觉自己接近了——至少是在地理位置上——那股黑暗力量的核心，而我这一代人正是在它的阴影之下成长的。在比克瑙，那是一个阴湿的午后，我站在毒气室的残砖碎瓦前——如今它奇异地被人遗忘了，荒废了——从德国人当年将它炸毁，赶在红军到来前逃之夭夭的那天起，这里几乎就再没有被人动过。如今它只是一堆湿漉漉的、破碎的水泥板，暴露在波兰严酷的气候中，一年更比一年残破。这处遗址应该被保护起来吗？应该在它的头顶上建起一个有机玻璃穹顶，把它保留下来，让我们的子孙后代得以亲眼目睹这里吗？还是说，我们就应该让它慢慢地、自然地朽烂瓦解，化作尘土？在我看来，这个沉重的问题象征着一个更大的两难抉择。这样的记忆应该如何保存？玻璃穹顶会将这些邪恶与苦难的遗迹化作波澜不惊的博物馆展品吗？我们应该选择哪些记忆？何时反倒不如忘却，轻装前行？

那年我四十四岁。在此之前，我一直将二战以及那场战争的恐怖与荣耀看作是我父母那一代人的。但此时此刻，我忽然意识到，要不了多久，许多亲眼见证了这些重大事件的人就将离开人世了。然后呢？记忆的重担就会落在我这一代人身上吗？我们没有经历过战争岁月，但抚养我们长大的父母们——他们的人生都被这场战争打上了不可磨灭的印记。而我——如今是一个向大众讲述故事的人——我是否肩负着一项迄今为止我都尚未意识到的责任呢？这责任是否就是向我们的后代尽己所能地传递我们父母辈的记忆与教训？

此后不久，我在东京的一群听众面前做了一次演讲，一位听众向我提问——这问题我经常碰到——接下来我打算写什么。接着，提问者更加明确地指出，我的作品经常写那些经历过社会与政治巨变的个体，当这些人物回顾人生时，总是挣扎着试图接纳自己那些阴暗的、耻辱的记忆。她问道，我未来的作品会继续涉猎这一领域吗？

我发现自己给出的是一个没有准备的回答。是的，我说，我经常写那些在遗忘与记忆之间挣扎的个体。但未来，我真正想写的故事是一个国家或一个群体是如何面对同样的问题的。国家记忆与遗忘的方式也与个体相似吗？还是说，两者有着本质的区别？国家的记忆究竟是什么？保存在哪里？又是如何被塑造、被操纵的？是否在某些时刻，遗忘是终结冤冤相报、阻止社会分裂瓦解、陷入战乱的唯一途径？而另一方面，稳定、自由的国家能否真的建立在蓄意的遗忘与正义的缺席之上？我听到自己对提问者说，我想要找到一个写出这些主题的途径，但不幸的是，我暂时恐怕还办不到。

*

二〇〇一年初的一个晚上，在北伦敦我们家（我们这时的居所）漆黑的客厅里，洛娜和我开始观看一部一九三四年霍华德·霍克斯执导的电影，片名叫做《二十世纪》（电影是录在一盘VHS录像带上的，画质尚可)。我们很快发现，片名指的并非是我们此刻刚刚告别的那个世纪，而是指那个年代非常出名的一列联结纽约与芝加哥的豪华列车。你们当中一定有人知道，这部电影是一出快节奏的喜剧，场景大部分都是在列车上，讲的是一个百老汇的制片人越来越绝望地试图阻止自己的头牌女演员转投好莱坞,踏上影星路。电影的压轴戏是约翰·巴里莫尔那令人叫绝的喜剧表演，他是那个时代最伟大的演员之一。他的面部表情，他的手势，他吐出的每一句台词，无不层层浸染出讽刺、矛盾与荒诞，而这一切背后的则是一个沉溺于自大狂与自吹自擂之中的男人。从许多方面来看，这都是精彩绝伦的表演。然而，随着影片的展开，我发现自己并没有被触动，这很奇怪。

我起初对此百思不得其解。通常来讲，我喜欢巴里莫尔，也很痴迷于霍华德·霍克斯这一时期执导的其他几部电影，比如《女友礼拜五》和《唯有天使生双翼》。后来，当电影放到差不多一个小时的时候，一个简单的、电光石火般的想法闪过我的脑海。不论是在小说、电影还是戏剧中，许多生动鲜活、十分可信的人物都没能触动我，其中的原因就在于，这些人物并没有与作品中的其他人物通过任何有意义的人际关系相联结。紧接着，下一个想法就跳到了我自己的创作上来：如果我不再关注我的人物，转而关注我的人物关系，那会怎样？

随着列车哐当哐当地一路向西，约翰·巴里莫尔变得越来越歇斯底里，我不禁想起了

E·M·福斯特那著名的二维人物与三维人物区分法。故事中的某个人物，他说过，只有在“令人信服地超出我们的意料”时，才能够变得三维。只有这样，他们才能“圆满”起来。但是，我此刻不禁思考，如果一个人物是三维的，但他或她所有的人际关系却并非如此，那又会怎样？同样是在那个讲座系列中，福斯特还作了一个幽默形象的比喻：要用一把镊子将小说的情节夹出，就像夹住一条蠕虫那样，举到灯光下仔细审视。我能否也作一次类似的审视，将任何一个故事中纵横交错的人物关系举到灯光下呢？我能否将这一方法应用到我自己的作品中——应用到我已完成的或正在规划的故事中？比如说，我可以审视一对师徒间的关系。这里有没有体现出任何深刻的、新鲜的东西？还是说，我看得愈久，就愈觉得这显然只是一种陈词滥调，已经在几百个平庸的故事中屡见不鲜？再比如说，两个相互较劲的朋友间的关系：它是否是动态的？是否能引发情感共鸣？是否在发展演化？是否令人信服地出人意料？是否三维？我突然觉得，我更好地理解了为什么我过去的作品中有这样那样的失败之处，尽管我也曾拼了命地想要弥补。我眼睛依然盯着约翰·巴里莫尔，脑子里却浮出一个想法：所有的好故事——不管它们的叙述模式是激进还是传统——都必须包含某些对我们有重要意义的关系，某些触动我们，让我们莞尔、让我们愤怒、让我们惊讶的关系。也许，在未来，如果我能够更多地关注我笔下的关系，我的人物就无需我再操心了。

我说出这席话时忽然想到，也许我着力阐述的这一点对你们而言本来就是显而易见的。但我能说的就是，这一发现在我写作生涯中可谓姗姗来迟，而我如今将这视为一个转折点，与我今天向你们讲述的其他关口同样重要。从那时起，我开始以一种截然不同的方法构建小说。比如说，我在创作长篇《莫失莫忘》时，我一开始思考的就是处于故事核心的那组三角关系，然后再是从这组关系发散开去的其他关系。

*

作家生涯中的重要转折点就是这样的——也许其他的职业生涯也是如此。它们时常是一些小小的、并不光鲜的时刻。它们是无声的、私密的启示火花。它们并不常见，而当它们到来时，也许没有号角齐鸣，也没有导师和同事的背书。它们时常不得不与另一些更响亮也似乎更急切的要求相竞争。有时，它们所揭示的会与主流观念相悖。但当它们到来时，我们一定要认识到它们的意义。不然的话，它们就会从你的指缝中流失。

我一直在这里强调那些细小的、私密的东西，因为本质上讲，这就是我工作的内容。一个人在一个安静的房间里写作，试图和另一个人建立联结，而那个人也在另一个安静的——也许不那么安静的房间里阅读。小说可以娱乐，有时也可以传授观点或是主张观点。但对我来说，最重要的一点在于，小说可以传递感受；在于它们诉诸的是我们作为人类所共享的东西——超越国界与阻隔的东西。许多庞大光鲜的产业都是围绕小说建立的——图书业、电影业、电视业、戏剧业。但最终，小说是一个人对另一个人的诉说。这就是我对于小说的感受。你们能够理解我的话吗？你们也是如此感受的吗？

*

于是，我们来到了当下。最近，我忽然醒悟到，多年来我一直生活在一个虚妄的肥皂泡中。我未能注意到我周围许多人的挫折与焦虑。我意识到，我的世界——一个文明、振奋的地方，满是爱开玩笑、思想开明的人——事实上比我想象的要小得多。二〇一六年，这一年在欧洲与美国发生了许多出人意料——于我而言也是令人沮丧的政治事件，全球发生了多起令人毛骨悚然的恐怖袭击。我从孩提时代起就理所当然地以为，自由主义—人本主义价值观前进的脚步不可阻挡，但二〇一六年的这一切都迫使我承认，也许我的想法只是一个幻觉。

我们这代人是乐观的一代。为什么？因为我们看着我们的长辈将欧洲从一片满是极权国家、种族清洗与史无前例的大屠杀的大陆，变成了一块人人羡慕、自由民主国家在几乎没有边界的友谊中共存的乐土。我们看着旧殖民帝国连同那些支撑它们的可恨观念一道在全世界土崩瓦解。我们看着女权主义、同性恋权利与抗击种族主义的多条战线高奏凯歌，齐头并进。我们在资本主义与共产主义猛烈对抗的背景中长大——一场意识形态的对抗与军事的对抗，最终却看到了我们许多人眼中的大团圆结局。

而此刻，回首往事，推倒柏林墙后的那个年代更像是骄傲自满的年代，错失良机的年代。我们坐视惊人的不平等——财富与机遇的不平等——在国家间与国家内部扩大。而二〇〇三年对伊拉克灾难性的入侵行动以及二〇〇八年那场丑恶的金融危机爆发后强加在普通人民身上的长期紧缩政策——尤其是这两起事件将我们推向了当下这个极右思潮与狭隘民族主义泛滥的局面。种族主义——不论是以其传统形式，还是以其营销更加得力的现代化形式——再次沉渣泛起，在我们文明的街道下蠢蠢欲动，就像一头被掩埋的巨兽正在苏醒。而此刻，我们似乎缺乏任何能将我们团结起来的进步事业。恰恰相反，甚至是在富裕的西方民主国家内，我们也正在分裂成彼此对立的不同阵营，为了争夺资源和权力而斗得天昏地暗。

与此同时，科学、技术与医学的重大突破向人类提出的挑战已经近在眼前了——还是说，已经到了眼前？新基因技术——比如基因编辑技术CRISPR——以及人工智能和机器人技术的进步都将为我们带来惊人的、足以拯救生命的收益，但同时也可能制造出野蛮的、类似种族隔离制度的精英统治社会以及严重的失业问题，甚至连那些眼下的专业精英也不能从中幸免。

就这样，我，一个已年过花甲的男人，揉着

双眼，试图在一片迷雾中，辨识出一些轮廓——那是一个直到昨天我才察觉其存在的世界。我，一个倦态已现的作家，来自智力上倦态已现的那一代人，现在还能打起精神，看一看这个陌生的地方吗？我还能拿出什么有所帮助的东西来，在当下社会挣扎适应巨变之际，为即将到来的争论、斗争与战争提供另一个视角，剖出另一些情感层面？

我必须继续前行，尽己所能。因为我依然相信，文学很重要，尤其是在我们渡过眼下这个难关的过程中。但我也期盼年轻一代的作家鼓舞我们，引领我们。这是他们的时代，他们会有我所缺乏的知识与直觉。在书本、电影院、电视与剧院的世界中，今天我看到了敢于冒险、激动人心的人才——四十岁、三十岁、二十岁的男男女女们。因此，我很乐观。我又有什么理由不乐观呢?

但最后，请允许我发起一项呼吁——如果你们愿意的话，就让这成为我作为诺贝尔奖得主的呼吁！要让整个世界走上正轨并不是一件易事，但至少让我们先思考一下该如何安排我们这个小小的角落，这个“文学”角落——在这里，我们阅读书籍，创作书籍，出版书籍，推荐书籍，谴责书籍，给书籍颁奖。如果我们想在这世事难料的未来中发挥重要的作用，如果我们想让今日和明日的作家发挥出最大能力，我相信我们必须更加多元化。我的意思有两层。

首先，我们必须拓展我们一般意义上的文学

界，囊括更多的声音，第一世界文化精英的舒适区以外的声音。我们必须更加勉力地搜寻，从迄今为止尚不为人所知的文学文化中发现宝石，不论那些作家是生活在遥远的国度还是生活在我们自己的社群中。其次，我们必须格外小心，不要将“何谓优秀文学”定义得过于狭隘或保守。下一代人定会用各式各样崭新的，有时甚至令人晕头转向的方法来讲述重大的、绝妙的故事。我们必须对他们保持开放的心态，尤其是在涉及体裁与形式的问题上，这样我们才能培养、拔擢他们中的佼佼者。在一个危险的、日益分裂的时代，我们必须倾听。好的创作与好的阅读可以打破壁垒。我们也许还可以发现一种新思想，一个人文主义的伟大愿景，团结在它的旗下。

对于瑞典文学院、诺贝尔基金会，以及瑞典人民——多年来，正是他们让诺贝尔奖成为了我们全人类努力谋求的“善”的一个闪亮象征——我在此呈上我的谢意。

Kazuo Ishiguro Nobel Lecture

My Twentieth Century Evening — and Other Small Breakthroughs

If you'd come across me in the autumn of 1979, you might have had some difficulty placing me, socially or even racially. I was then 24 years old. My features would have looked Japanese, but unlike most Japanese men seen in Britain in those days, I had hair down to my shoulders, and a drooping bandit-style moustache. The only accent discernible in my speech was that of someone brought up in the southern counties of England, inflected at times by the languid, already dated vernacular of the Hippie era. If we'd got talking, we might have discussed the Total Footballers of Holland, or Bob Dylan's latest album, or perhaps the year I'd just spent working with homeless people in London. Had you mentioned Japan, asked me about its culture, you might even have detected a trace of impatience enter my manner as I declared my ignorance on the grounds that I hadn't set foot in that country – not even for a holiday – since leaving it at the age of five.

That autumn I'd arrived with a rucksack, a guitar and a portable typewriter in Buxton, Norfolk – a small English village with an old water mill and flat farm fields all around it. I'd come to this place because I'd been accepted on a one-year postgraduate Creative Writing course at the University of East Anglia. The university was ten miles away, in the cathedral town of Norwich, but I had no car and my only way of getting there was by means of a bus service that operated just once in the morning, once at lunch-time and once in the evening. But this, I was soon to discover, was no great hardship: I was rarely required at the university more than twice a week. I'd rented a room in a small house owned by a man in his thirties whose wife had just left him. No doubt, for him, the house was filled with the ghosts of his wrecked dreams – or perhaps he just wanted to avoid me; in any case, I didn't set eyes on him for days on end. In other words, after the frenetic life I'd been leading in London, here I was, faced with an unusual amount of quiet and solitude in which to transform myself into a writer.

In fact, my little room was not unlike the classic writer's garret. The ceilings sloped claustrophobically – though if I stood on tip-toes I had a view, from my one window, of ploughed fields stretching away into the distance. There was a small table, the surface of which my typewriter and a desk lamp took up almost entirely. On the floor, instead of a bed, there was a large rectangular piece of industrial foam that would cause me to sweat in my sleep, even during the bitterly cold Norfolk nights.

It was in this room that I carefully examined the two short stories I'd written over the summer, wondering if they were good enough to submit to my new classmates. (We were, I knew, a class of six, meeting once every two weeks.) At that point in my life I'd written little else of note in the way of prose fiction, having earned my place on the course with a radio play rejected by the BBC. In fact, having previously made firm plans to become a rock star by the time I was twenty, my literary ambitions had only recently made themselves known to me. The two stories I was now scrutinising had been written in something of a panic, in response to the news that I'd been accepted on the university course. One was about a macabre suicide pact, the other about street fights in Scotland, where I'd spent some time as a community worker. They were not so good. I started another story, about an adolescent who poisons his cat, set like the others in present day Britain. Then one night, during my third or fourth week in that little room, I found myself writing, with a new and urgent intensity, about Japan – about Nagasaki, the city of my birth, during the last days of the Second World War.

This, I should point out, came as something of a surprise to me. Today, the prevailing atmosphere is such that it's virtually an instinct for an aspiring young writer with a mixed cultural heritage to explore his 'roots' in his work. But that was far from the case then. We were still a few years away from the explosion of 'multicultural' literature in Britain.

Salman Rushdie was an unknown with one out-of-print novel to his name. Asked to name the leading young British novelist of the day, people might have mentioned Margaret Drabble; of older writers, Iris Murdoch, Kingsley Amis, William Golding, Anthony Burgess, John Fowles. Foreigners like Gabriel García Márquez, Milan Kundera or Borges were read only in tiny numbers, their names meaningless even to keen readers.

Such was the literary climate of the day that when I finished that first Japanese story, for all my sense of having discovered an important new direction, I began immediately to wonder if this departure shouldn't be viewed as a self-indulgence; if I shouldn't quickly return to more 'normal' subject matter. It was only after considerable hesitation I began to show the story around, and I remain to this day profoundly grateful to my fellow students, to my tutors, Malcolm Bradbury and Angela Carter, and to the novelist Paul Bailey – that year the university's writer-in-residence – for their determinedly encouraging response. Had they been less positive, I would probably never again have written about Japan. As it was, I returned to my room and wrote and wrote. Throughout the winter of 1979-80, and well into the spring, I spoke to virtually no-one aside from the other five students in my class, the village grocer from whom I bought the breakfast cereals and lamb kidneys on which I existed, and my girlfriend, Lorna, (today my wife) who'd come to visit me every second weekend. It wasn't a balanced life, but in those four or five months I managed to complete one half of my first novel, A Pale View of Hills – set also in Nagasaki, in the years of recovery after the dropping of the atomic bomb. I can remember occasionally during this period tinkering with some ideas for short stories not set in Japan, only to find my interest waning rapidly.

Those months were crucial for me, in so far as without them I'd probably never have become a writer. Since then, I've often looked back and asked:

what was going on with me? What was all this peculiar energy? My conclusion has been that just at that point in my life, I'd become engaged in an urgent act of preservation. To explain this, I'll need to go back a little.

*

I had come to England, aged five, with my parents and sister in April 1960, to the town of Guildford, Surrey, in the affluent 'stockbroker belt' thirty miles south of London. My father was a research scientist, an oceanographer who'd come to work for the British government. The machine he went on to invent, incidentally, is today part of the permanent collection at the Science Museum in London.

The photographs taken shortly after our arrival show an England from a vanished era. Men wear woollen V-neck pullovers with ties, cars still have running boards and a spare wheel on the back. The Beatles, the sexual revolution, student protests, 'multiculturalism' were all round the corner, but it's hard to believe the England our family first encountered even suspected it. To meet a foreigner from France or Italy was remarkable enough – never mind one from Japan.

Our family lived in a cul-de-sac of twelve houses just

where the paved roads ended and the countryside began. It was less than a five minute stroll to the local farm and the lane down which rows of cows trudged back and forth between fields. Milk was delivered by horse and cart. A common sight I remember vividly from my first days in England was that of hedgehogs – the cute, spiky, nocturnal creatures then numerous in that country – squashed by car wheels during the night, left in the morning dew, tucked neatly by the roadside, awaiting collection by the refuse men.

All our neighbours went to church, and when I went to play with their children, I noticed they said a small prayer before eating.

I attended Sunday school, and before long was singing in the church choir, becoming, aged ten, the first Japanese Head Chorister seen in Guildford. I went to the local primary school – where I was the only non-English child, quite possibly in the entire history of that school – and from when I was eleven, I travelled by train to my grammar school in a neighbouring town, sharing the carriage each morning with ranks of men in pinstripe suits and bowler hats, on their way to their offices in London.

By this stage, I'd become thoroughly trained in the manners expected of English middle-class boys in those days. When visiting a friend's house, I knew I should stand to attention the instant an adult wandered into the room; I learned that during a meal I had to ask permission before getting down from the table. As the only foreign boy in the neighbourhood, a kind of local fame followed me around. Other children knew who I was before I met them. Adults who were total strangers to me sometimes addressed me by name in the street or in the local store.

When I look back to this period, and remember it was less than twenty years from the end of a world war in which the Japanese had been their bitter enemies, I'm amazed by the openness and instinctive generosity with which our family was accepted by this ordinary English community. The affection, respect and curiosity I retain to this day for that generation of Britons who came through the Second World War, and built a remarkable new welfare state in its aftermath, derive significantly from my personal experiences from those years.

But all this time, I was leading another life at home with my Japanese parents. At home there were different rules, different expectations, a different language. My parents' original intention had been that we return to Japan after a year, perhaps two. In fact, for our first eleven years in England, we were in a perpetual state of going back 'next year'. As a result, my parents' outlook remained that of visitors, not of immigrants. They'd often exchange observations about the curious customs of the natives without feeling any onus to adopt them. And for a long time the assumption remained that I would return to live my adult life in Japan, and efforts were made to keep up the Japanese side of my education. Each month a parcel arrived from Japan, containing the previous month's comics, magazines and educational digests, all of which I devoured eagerly. These parcels stopped arriving some time in my teens – perhaps after my grandfather's death – but my parents' talk of old friends, relatives, episodes from their lives in Japan all kept up a steady supply of images and impressions. And then I always had my own store of memories – surprisingly vast and clear: of my grandparents, of favourite toys I'd left behind, the traditional Japanese house we'd lived in (which I can even today reconstruct in my mind room by room), my kindergarten, the local tram stop, the fierce dog that lived by the bridge, the chair in the barber's shop specially adapted for small boys with a car steering wheel fixed in front of the big mirror.

What this all amounted to was that as I was growing up, long before I'd ever thought to create fictional worlds in prose, I was busily constructing in my mind a richly detailed place called 'Japan' – a place to which I in some way belonged, and from which I drew a certain sense of my identity and my confidence. The fact that I'd never physically returned to Japan during that time only served to make my own vision of the country more vivid and personal.

Hence the need for preservation. For by the time I reached my mid-twenties – though I never clearly articulated this at the time – I was coming to realise certain key things. I was starting to accept that 'my' Japan perhaps didn't much correspond to any place I could go to on a plane; that the way of life of which my parents talked, that I remembered from my early childhood, had largely vanished during the 1960s and 1970s; that in any case, the Japan that existed in my head might always have been an emotional construct put together by a child out of memory, imagination and speculation. And perhaps most significantly, I'd come to realise that with each year I grew older, this Japan of mine – this precious place I'd grown up with – was getting fainter and fainter.

I'm now sure that it was this feeling, that 'my' Japan was unique and at the same time terribly fragile – something not open to verification from outside – that drove me on to work in that small room in Norfolk. What I was doing was getting down on paper that world's special colours, mores, etiquettes, its dignity, its shortcomings, everything I'd ever thought about the place, before they faded forever from my mind. It was my wish to re-build my Japan in fiction, to make it safe, so that I could thereafter point to a book and say: 'Yes, there's my Japan, inside there.'

*

Spring 1983, three and a half years later. Lorna and I were now in London, lodging in two rooms at the top of a tall narrow house, which itself stood on a hill at one of the highest points of the city. There was a television mast nearby and when we tried to listen to records on our turntable, ghostly broadcasting voices would intermittently invade our speakers. Our living room had no sofa or armchair, but two mattresses on the floor covered with cushions. There was also a large table on which I wrote during the day, and where we had dinner at night. It wasn't luxurious, but we liked living there. I'd published my first novel the year before, and I'd also written a screenplay for a short film soon to be broadcast on British television.

I'd been for a time reasonably proud of my first novel, but by that spring, a niggling sense of dissatisfaction had set in. Here was the problem. My first novel and my first TV screenplay were too similar. Not in subject matter, but in method and style. The more I looked at it, the more my novel resembled a screenplay – dialogue plus directions. This was okay up to a point, but my wish now was to write fiction that could work properly only on the page. Why write a novel if it was going to offer more or less the same experience someone could get by turning on a television? How could written fiction hope to survive against the might of cinema and television if it didn't offer something unique, something the other forms couldn't do?

Around this time, I came down with a virus and spent a few days in bed. When I came out of the worst of it, and I didn't feel like sleeping all the time, I discovered that the heavy object, whose presence amidst my bedclothes had been annoying me for some time, was in fact a copy of the first volume of Marcel Proust's Remembrance of Things Past (as the title was then translated). There it was, so I started to read it. My still fevered condition was perhaps a factor, but I became completely riveted by the Overture and Combray sections. I read them over and over. Quite aside from the sheer beauty of these passages, I became thrilled by the means by which Proust got one episode to lead into the next. The ordering of events and scenes didn't follow the usual demands of chronology, nor those of a linear plot. Instead, tangential thought associations, or the vagaries of memory seemed to move the writing from one episode to the next. Sometimes I found myself wondering: why had these two seemingly unrelated moments been placed side by side in the narrator's mind? I could suddenly see an exciting, freer way of composing my second novel; one that could produce richness on the page and offer inner movements impossible to capture on any screen. If I could go from one passage to the next according to the narrator's thought associations and drifting memories, I could compose in something like the way an abstract painter might choose to place shapes and colours around a canvas. I could place a scene from two days ago right beside one from twenty years earlier, and ask the reader to ponder the relationship between the two. In such a way, I began to think, I might suggest the many layers of self-deception and denial that shrouded any person's view of their own self and of their past.

*

March 1988. I was 33 years old. We now had a sofa and I was lying across it, listening to a Tom Waits album. The previous year, Lorna and I had bought our own house in an unfashionable but pleasant part of South London, and in this house, for the first time, I had my own study. It was small, and didn't have a door, but I was thrilled to spread my papers around and not have to clear them away at the end of each day. And in that study – or so I believed – I'd just finished my third novel. It was my first not to have a Japanese setting – my personal Japan having been made less fragile by the writing of my previous novels. In fact my new book, to be called The Remains of the Day, seemed English in the extreme – though not, I hoped, in the manner of many British authors of the older generation. I'd been careful not to assume, as I felt many of them did, that my readers were all English, with native familiarity of English nuances and preoccupations. By then, writers like Salman Rushdie and V.S. Naipaul had forged the way for a more international, outward-looking British literature, one that didn't claim any centrality or automatic importance for Britain. Their writing was post-colonial in the widest sense. I wanted, like them, to write 'international' fiction that could easily cross cultural and linguistic boundaries, even while writing a story set in what seemed a peculiarly English world. My version of England would be a kind of mythical one, whose outlines, I believed, were already present in the imaginations of many people around the world, including those who had never visited the country.

The story I'd just finished was about an English butler who realises, too late in his life, that he has lived his life by the wrong values; and that he's given his best years to serving a Nazi sympa-thizer; that by failing to take moral and political responsibility for his life, he has in some profound sense wasted that life. And more: that in his bid to become the perfect servant, he has forbidden himself to love, or be loved by, the one woman he cares for.

I'd read through my manuscript several times, and I'd been reasonably satisfied. Still, there was a niggling feeling that something was missing.

Then, as I say, there I was, in our house one evening, on our sofa, listening to Tom Waits. And Tom Waits began to sing a song called 'Ruby's Arms'. Perhaps some of you know it. (I even thought about singing it to you at this point, but I've changed my mind.) It's a ballad about a man, possibly a soldier, leaving his lover asleep in bed. It's the early morning, he goes down the road, gets on a train. Nothing unusual in that. But the song is delivered in the voice of a gruff American hobo utterly unaccustomed to revealing his deeper emotions. And there comes a moment, midway through the song, when the singer tells us that his heart is breaking. The moment is almost unbearably moving because of the tension between the sentiment itself and the huge resistance that's obviously been overcome to declare it. Tom Waits sings the line with cathartic magnificence, and you feel a lifetime of tough-guy stoicism crumbling in the face of overwhelming sadness.

As I listened to Tom Waits, I realised what I'd still left to do. I'd unthinkingly made the decision, somewhere way back, that my English butler would maintain his emotional defences, that he'd manage to hide behind them, from himself and his reader, to the very end. Now I saw I had to reverse that decision. Just for one moment, towards the end of my story, a moment I'd have to choose carefully, I had to make his armour crack. I had to allow a vast and tragic yearning to be glimpsed underneath.

I should say here that I have, on a number of other occasions, learned crucial lessons from the voices of singers. I refer here less to the lyrics being sung, and more to the actual singing. As we know, a human voice in song is capable of expressing an unfathomably complex blend of feelings. Over the years, specific aspects of my writing have been influenced by, among others, Bob Dylan, Nina Simone, Emmylou Harris, Ray Charles, Bruce Springsteen, Gillian Welch and my friend and collaborator Stacey Kent. Catching something in their voices, I've said to myself: 'Ah yes, that's it. That's what I need to capture in that scene. Something very close to that.' Often it's an emotion

I can't quite put into words, but there it is, in the singer's voice, and now I've been given something to aim for.

*

In October 1999 I was invited by the German poet Christoph Heubner on behalf of the International Auschwitz Committee to spend a few days visiting the former concentration camp. My accommodation was at the Auschwitz Youth Meeting Centre on the road between the first Auschwitz camp and the Birkenau death camp two miles away. I was shown around these sites and met, informally, three survivors. I felt I'd come close, geographically at least, to the heart of the dark force under whose shadow my generation had grown up. At Birkenau, on a wet afternoon, I stood before the rubbled remains of the gas chambers – now strangely neglected and unattended – left much as the Germans had left them after blowing them up and fleeing the Red Army. They were now just damp, broken slabs, exposed to the harsh Polish climate, deteriorating year by year. My hosts talked about their dilemma. Should these remains be protected? Should perspex domes be built to cover them over, to preserve them for the eyes of succeeding generations? Or should they be allowed, slowly and naturally, to rot away to nothing? It seemed to me a powerful metaphor for a larger dilemma. How were such memories to be preserved? Would the glass domes transform these relics of evil and suffering into tame museum exhibits? What should we choose to remember? When is it better to forget and move on?

I was 44 years old. Until then I'd considered the Second World War, its horrors and its triumphs, as belonging to my parents' generation. But now it occurred to me that before too long, many who had witnessed those huge events at first hand would not be alive. And what then? Did the burden of remembering fall to my own generation? We hadn't experienced the war years, but we'd at least been brought up by parents whose lives had been indelibly shaped by them. Did I, now, as a public teller of stories, have a duty I'd hitherto been unaware of? A duty to pass on, as best I could, these memories and lessons from our parents' generation to the one after our own?

A little while later, I was speaking before an audience in Tokyo, and a questioner from the floor asked, as is common, what I might work on next. More specifically, the questioner pointed out that my books had often concerned individuals who'd lived through times of great social and political upheaval, and who then looked back over their lives and struggled to come to terms with their darker, more shameful memories. Would my future books, she asked, continue to cover a similar territory?

I found myself giving a quite unprepared answer. Yes, I said, I'd often written about such individuals struggling between forgetting and remembering. But in the future, what I really wished to do was to write a story about how a nation or a community faced these same questions. Does a nation remember and forget in much the same way as an individual does? Or are there important differences? What exactly are the memories of a nation? Where are they kept? How are they shaped and controlled? Are there times when forgetting is the only way to stop cycles of violence, or to stop a society disintegrating into chaos or war? On the other hand, can stable, free nations really be built on foundations of wilful amnesia and frustrated justice? I heard myself telling the questioner that I wanted to find a way to write about these things, but that for the moment, unfortunately, I couldn't think how I'd do it.

*

One evening in early 2001, in the darkened front room of our house in North London (where we were by then living), Lorna and I began to watch, on a reasonable quality VHS tape, a 1934 Howard Hawks film called Twentieth Century. The film's title, we soon discovered, referred not to the century we'd then just left behind, but to a famous luxury train of the era connecting New York and Chicago. As some of you will know, the film is a fast-paced comedy, set largely on the train, concerning a Broadway producer who, with increasing desperation, tries to prevent his leading actress going to Hollywood to become a movie star. The film is built around a huge comic performance by John Barrymore, one of the great actors of his day. His facial expressions, his gestures, almost every line he utters come layered with ironies, contradictions, the grotesqueries of a man drowning in egocentricity and self-dramatisation. It is in many ways a brilliant performance. Yet, as the film continued to unfold, I found myself curiously uninvolved. This puzzled me at first. I usually liked Barrymore, and was a big enthusiast for Howard Hawks's other films from this period – such as His Girl Friday and Only Angels Have Wings. Then, around the film's one hour mark, a simple, striking idea came into my head. The reason why so many vivid, undeniably convincing characters in novels, films and plays so often failed to touch me was because these characters didn't connect to any of the other characters in an interesting human relationship. And immediately, this next thought came regarding my own work: What if I stopped worrying about my characters and worried instead about my relationships?

As the train rattled farther west and John Barrymore became ever more hysterical, I thought about E.M. Forster's famous distinction between three-dimensional and two-dimensional characters. A character in a story became three-dimensional, he'd said, by virtue of the fact that they 'surprised us convincingly'. It was in so doing they became 'rounded'. But what, I now wondered, if a character was three-dimensional, while all his or her relationships were not? Elsewhere in that same lecture series, Forster had used a humorous image, of extracting the storyline out of a novel with a pair of forceps and holding it up, like a wriggling worm, for examination under the light. Couldn't I perform a similar exercise and hold up to the light the various relationships that criss-cross any story? Could I do this with my own work – to stories I'd completed and ones I was planning? I could look at, say, this mentor-pupil relationship. Does it say something insightful and fresh? Or now that I was staring at it, does it become obvious it's a tired stereotype, identical to those found in hundreds of mediocre stories? Or this relationship between two competitive friends: is it dynamic? Does it have emotional resonance? Does it evolve? Does it surprise convincingly? Is it three-dimensional? I suddenly felt I understood better why in the past various aspects of my work had failed, despite my applying desperate remedies. The thought came to me – as I continued to stare at John Barrymore – that all good stories, never mind how radical or traditional their mode of telling, had to contain relationships that are important to us; that move us, amuse us, anger us, surprise us. Perhaps in future, if I attended more to my relationships, my characters would take care of themselves.

It occurs to me as I say this that I might be making a point here that has always been plainly obvious to you. But all I can say is that it was an idea that came to me surprisingly late in my writing life, and I see it now as a turning point, comparable with the others I've been describing to you today. From then on, I began to build my stories in a different way. When writing my novel Never Let Me Go, for instance, I set off from the start by thinking about its central relationships triangle, and then the other relationships that fanned out from it.

*

Important turning points in a writer's career – perhaps in many kinds of career – are like these. Often, they are small, scruffy moments. They are quiet, private sparks of revelation. They don't come often, and when they do, they may well come without fanfare, unendorsed by mentors or colleagues. They must often compete for attention with louder, seemingly more urgent demands. Sometimes what they reveal may go against the grain of prevailing wisdom. But when they come, it's important to be able to recognise them for what they are. Or they'll slip through your hands.

I've been emphasising here the small and the private, because essentially that's what my work is about. One person writing in a quiet room, trying to connect with another person, reading in another quiet – or maybe not so quiet – room. Stories can entertain, sometimes teach or argue a point. But for me the essential thing is that they communicate feelings. That they appeal to what we share as human beings across our borders and divides. There are large glamorous industries around stories; the book industry, the movie industry, the television industry, the theatre industry. But in the end, stories are about one person saying to another: This is the way it feels to me. Can you understand what I'm saying? Does it also feel this way to you?

*

So we come to the present. I woke up recently to the realisation I'd been living for some years in a bubble. That I'd failed to notice the frustration and anxieties of many people around me. I realised that my world –

a civilised, stimulating place filled with ironic, liberal-minded people – was in fact much smaller than I'd ever imagined. 2016, a year of surprising – and for me depressing – political events in Europe and in America, and of sickening acts of terrorism all around the globe, forced me to acknowledge that the unstoppable advance of liberal-humanist values I'd taken for granted since childhood may have been an illusion.

I'm part of a generation inclined to optimism, and why not? We watched our elders successfully transform Europe from a place of totalitarian regimes, genocide and historically unprecedented carnage to a much-envied region of liberal democracies living in near-borderless friendship. We watched the old colonial empires crumble around the world together with the reprehensible assumptions that underpinned them. We saw significant progress in feminism, gay rights and the battles on several fronts against racism. We grew up against a backdrop of the great clash – ideological and military – between capitalism and communism, and witnessed what many of us believed to be a happy conclusion.

But now, looking back, the era since the fall of the Berlin Wall seems like one of complacency, of opportunities lost. Enormous inequalities – of wealth and opportunity – have been allowed to grow, between nations and within nations. In particular, the disastrous invasion of Iraq in 2003, and the long years of austerity policies imposed on ordinary people following the scandalous economic crash of 2008, have brought us to a present in which Far Right ideologies and tribal nationalisms proliferate. Racism, in its traditional forms and in its modernised, better-marketed versions, is once again on the rise, stirring beneath our civilised streets like a buried monster awakening. For the moment we seem to lack any progressive cause to unite us. Instead, even in the wealthy democracies of the West, we're fracturing into rival camps from which to compete bitterly for resources or power.

And around the corner – or have we already turned this corner? – lie the challenges posed by stunning breakthroughs in science, technology and medicine. New genetic technologies – such as the gene-editing technique CRISPR – and advances in Artificial Intelligence and robotics will bring us amazing, life-saving benefits, but may also create savage meritocracies that resemble apartheid, and massive unemployment, including to those in the current professional elites.

So here I am, a man in my sixties, rubbing my eyes

and trying to discern the outlines, out there in the mist, to this world I didn't suspect even existed until yesterday. Can I, a tired author, from an intellectually tired generation, now find the energy to look at this unfamiliar place? Do I have something left that might help to provide perspective, to bring emotional layers to the arguments, fights and wars that will come as societies struggle to adjust to huge changes?

I'll have to carry on and do the best I can. Because I still believe that literature is important, and will be particularly so as we cross this difficult terrain. But I'll be looking to the writers from the younger generations to inspire and lead us. This is their era, and they will have the knowledge and instinct about it that I will lack. In the worlds of books, cinema, TV and theatre I see today adventurous, exciting talents: women and men in their forties, thirties and twenties. So I am optimistic. Why shouldn't I be?

But let me finish by making an appeal – if you like, my Nobel appeal! It's hard to put the whole world to rights, but let us at least think about how we can prepare our own small corner of it, this corner of 'literature', where we read, write, publish, recommend, denounce and give awards to books. If we are to play an important role in this uncertain future, if we are to get the best from the writers of today and tomorrow, I believe we must become more diverse. I mean this in two particular senses.

Firstly, we must widen our common literary world to include many more voices from beyond our comfort zones of the elite first world cultures. We must search more energetically to discover the gems from what remain today unknown literary cultures, whether the writers live in far away countries or within our own communities. Second: we must take great care not to set too narrowly or conservatively our definitions of what constitutes good literature. The next generation will come with all sorts of new, sometimes bewildering ways to tell important and wonderful stories. We must keep our minds open to them, especially regarding genre and form, so that we can nurture and celebrate the best of them. In a time of dangerously increasing division, we must listen. Good writing and good reading will break down barriers. We may even find a new idea, a great humane vision, around which to rally.

To the Swedish Academy, the Nobel Foundation, and to the people of Sweden who down the years have made the Nobel Prize a shining symbol for the good we human beings strive for – I give my thanks.